ASCD | arias

SUCCESS WITH IEPs

*Solving Five Common
Implementation Challenges
in the Classroom*

Vicki **CARUANA**

Alexandria, VA USA

Website: www.ascd.org
E-mail: books@ascd.org

www.ascdarias.org

Printed in the United States of America. ASCD publications present a variety of viewpoints. The views expressed or implied in this book should not be interpreted as official positions of the Association.

PAPERBACK ISBN: 978-1-4166-2376-2   ASCD product #SF117047

Also available as an e-book (see Books in Print for the ISBNs).

Library of Congress Cataloging-in-Publication Data

Names: Caruana, Vicki, author.
Title: Success with IEPs : solving five common implementation challenges in the classroom / Vicki Caruana.
Description: Alexandria, Virginia : ASCD, [2017] | Includes bibliographical references.
Identifiers: LCCN 2016050064 | ISBN 9781416623762 (Paperback)
Subjects: LCSH: Individualized education programs--United States. | Learning
    disabled children--Education--United States.
Classification: LCC LC4019 .C37 2017 | DDC 371.9/043940973--dc23 LC record available at https://lccn.loc.gov/2016050064

25 24 23 22 21 20 19 18 17   1 2 3 4 5 6 7 8 9 10

ASCD | arias

SUCCESS WITH IEPs

*Solving Five Common
Implementation Challenges
in the Classroom*

Want to earn a free ASCD Arias e-book?
Your opinion counts! Please take 2–3 minutes to give
us your feedback on this publication. All survey
respondents will be entered into a drawing to
win an ASCD Arias e-book.

Please visit
www.ascd.org/ariasfeedback

Thank you!

Introduction

You survey your class roster during preservice and notice symbols next to the names of particular children. Your class list looks like an indecipherable code waiting to be broken. Maybe you learned some code-breaking techniques during teacher preparation; maybe you have a natural affinity as a cipher; maybe you only learned enough to know there is meaning in the code but not the meaning itself. Either way, you are responsible for ensuring a meaningful education for all of the students in your charge, whether or not they have a symbol next to their name.

At the intersection of No Child Left Behind and Individuals with Disabilities Education Improvement Act (IDEIA 2004) lies the instructional responsibility of the general education teacher to provide meaningful access to the general curriculum for students with disabilities in their classrooms (McNulty & Gloeckler, 2011). For more than a decade, the implementation of higher state standards for both teacher preparation and curriculum for preK–12 students has defined for us all the responsibility we hold for all children. Students with disabilities are expected to (1) be educated as much as possible alongside their peers without disabilities and (2) access the general education curriculum with appropriate supports (IDEIA, 2004). Because the most common placement for students with mild, high-incidence disabilities is the general education classroom, the teachers in this inclusive setting need to be prepared to be responsible for providing that access to the general curriculum.

During teacher preparation you may have taken an introduction to special education, inclusive education, or response to intervention (RtI) course that outlined the characteristics and needs of students with disabilities and ways in which you might differentiate your planning, instruction, and assessment for these students. You may have even been required to take and pass a certification exam in the area of special education in order to obtain a dual teaching license. You may have had neither of these experiences if you took an alternative route to teacher certification. Whatever preparation you have, you still may feel ill-equipped to ensure that you meet the needs of students with individualized education plan (IEPs) in your classroom (Samuels, 2013). This book outlines five things teachers who have success with IEPs do differently and practical insights, tips, and strategies for how you can achieve this same success with your IEPs.

Confidence is built on the foundation of competence. If you are uncertain of your ability to meet the needs of students on IEPs, this book is a great place to start. Once your competence increases, your confidence will increase. The principles and strategies in this book offer you a chance to fine-tune your practice as well as clarify some of the foggy ideas you may have about ensuring success for students with disabilities in your charge. Let's get started!

1. Realize the Full Scope of Your Role in the IEP Process

As the teacher, you are in a unique position to make the IEP process a success, but you will need to get a sense of how wide-ranging your role could potentially be. Not only will you be leading implementation, you may also find yourself asked to complete a mountain of paperwork, observe one of your students for specific behaviors, or even come up with other ways you can be an active, and not a passive, member of the IEP team. Such a broad range of responsibilities means that you need to know how to reflect on and maximize your influence. This includes taking a hard look at your own beliefs and biases, knowing what to look for as you observe the children's learning, and remaining an active participant in their learning.

Look at Your Own Beliefs and Biases

We all have biases. These biases tend to color our attitudes toward any particular individual, group, or topic. If you feel any apprehension about working with a student on an IEP, it can be due to several causes. It may be that you believe you have a lack of experience to work with these particular students. It may be that you are skeptical about inclusion (Cassady, 2011). It may be that you struggle with the nature or types of specific disabilities. It may also depend on what level of support you have from administration and other teachers. Whether you hold a positive or negative attitude toward having students with a variety of disabilities in your classroom, it's important to conscious of the fact that your attitudes translate into actions. Your sense of efficacy (competence) grows out of your confidence as well as your genuine concern for each child.

Avramidis, Bayliss, and Burden (2000) reported that teachers who did not fully agree with inclusion were less likely to differentiate instruction according to students' needs and were less confident that they could implement the required accommodations and requirements of an IEP. Unfortunately, when teachers have negative attitudes toward including students with disabilities in their classrooms, they may not provide the needed supports for those students. Often teachers are more positive about including students whose characteristics or needs are not as likely to require extra instructional or management skills from the teacher (Avramidis et al., 2000). Where are you on the Attitudes Toward Inclusion Scale (Figure 1)?

FIGURE 1: **Attitudes Toward Inclusion Scale**

Although you may have an accepting or even celebrating attitude toward working with students who have an IEP, you may not feel prepared to do so successfully. Efficacy is a combination of confidence plus competence.

One new teacher I once worked with, Megan, was painfully aware of the weight of the responsibility she held for the four students in her 5th grade class who had IEPs. She viewed their unique needs as puzzles to solve, not obstacles to her dream of a problem-free classroom. Immediately Megan took time to meet with the case manager of each child and map out a plan to ensure that both she and her students were on top of their IEP goals. She had a lot to learn, but she hoped her willingness would outweigh her inexperience. Megan read through each IEP and wondered how she would manage so many individual goals. As the year progressed, Megan began to understand how to better address Justin's reading comprehension struggles, Sarah's difficulty with remembering math facts, Kyle's organizational challenges, and Jacqueline's expressive language frustrations. Was it possible to meet each of their IEP goals? Megan knew that something is always better than nothing, so her willingness to try made a huge difference in the support she gave these students as they pursued their individual goals. At the end of the year, after Megan had targeted instruction to improving Sarah's memory of her multiplication facts, Sarah improved her retention from 5 percent to 65 percent mastery. Although the criteria of 85 percent was not met, the amount of growth is considered a success.

On the other hand, Carl, another young teacher I once worked with, looked at the fact that two of the students on his class roster had the IEP box checked and let out an audible sigh during his 6th grade level meeting. *Why can't I just focus on my content*? he wondered. Neither of these students were on grade level. How was he supposed to magically bring them up? Not only did Carl not feel up to the task, he was also concerned about how having these students in his class would affect his annual performance review. He saw them like flies in the ointment and not children in need of his teaching. Carl was a good teacher, and his students loved him. He made science come alive and his passion for all things earth and space make his class sought after. Instead of looking at the IEP needs of these two students as something he could apply the scientific problem solving method to, he saw it as something to avoid. He believed that his passion and good teaching was enough for any child to succeed and he didn't need help to ensure the success of Tara and Michael. Carl never even looked at their IEP goals. As a result, none of their goals were met that year.

An intolerant or even ambivalent attitude may mean that you may be more resistant to your role in the IEP process. It's important to conduct some self-reflection on this important part of your role. Although it is not always possible to meet every IEP goal by the end of the year, attending to the process will make a huge difference in how close your students get to their goals.

Understand the Nature and Type of the Disability

Perceptions and facts about specific disabilities are often at odds. Perceptions such as students with a learning disability are just not trying hard enough, students with an emotional or behavioral disorder are volatile, or students on the autism spectrum are difficult to manage are all perceptions not based on facts. They are, however, prevalent and have the potential to influence how you approach your work with students. If you don't understand the nature and type of the disability of the student for whom you are working on their IEP, then you won't provide the right performance information, instructional strategies, and ways to evaluate their progress.

Three areas that every teacher should know and understand about the range of disabilities that are represented in their classroom include characteristics and needs, recommended instructional strategies, and IEP considerations. For example, a common characteristic of a child with a specific learning disability in reading is comprehension. The student may need frequent practice with unfamiliar words (vocabulary) requiring the research-based strategy of explicit instruction (Archer & Hughes, 2011). This child's IEP should have goals targeting different subskills of reading comprehension with grade level texts. If you are unaware that poor reading comprehension is a common characteristic for students with a learning disability, and that their challenges include moving concepts from short- to long-term memory, then you will not plan appropriately to meet their needs.

The learning experiences you encountered during your teacher preparation may not be sufficient to help you discern the nature and type of each disability. To improve your knowledge and skills in these areas, do your own research and collaborate with the special education teachers in your school to learn more.

There are a variety of online resources to help teachers better work with students with disabilities. Your state offers the definitions of the different disability categories and the expected roles and responsibilities of teachers working with students, and the federal definitions and guidelines are provided through IDEIA. Bookmark both resources for future reference.

Another source of information is the special education teacher in your school, who can provide insight and practical tips to working successfully with your shared students. In addition, if not provided, you could and should request an IEP snapshot that will give you the most important information at a glance on a particular student (see the Encore, p. 51). Once you understand the nature and type of disability that your students are living with, you will be better able to fulfill your role and responsibilities in the IEP process.

Know How to Observe Special Education Students

Part of the IEP process is for teachers who interact with the student to provide data about their performance, whether academic or behavioral. This goes beyond calculating what reading level the student is on or how many math facts he has mastered. How the student engages with the content and the classroom environment are just as important. Behaviors exhibited during instruction or assessment are important to observe and record. Often you will be asked to describe your observations of a student's disability and its impact during your class. Whenever possible, you will be asked to provide specific examples, including the frequency and severity of symptoms displayed in your class. You will be expected to conduct these observations in a non-biased manner and provide the data gained from the observations to the child study team or IEP team. There are two main types of observations teachers will employ: naturalistic and systematic.

Naturalistic observation is the most common and often referred to as *anecdotal*. This type of observation focuses on directly observed occurrences in the classroom. When making an anecdotal or naturalistic observation, you should reserve judgment or interpretation of what you observe. This is a recording of events as they happen. One of the most commonly used forms of naturalistic observation is ABC (antecedent, behavior, and consequence). Figure 2 represents one naturalistic observation of a child's behavior in the classroom.

The second type of observation is *systematic observation*. The focus is on observing a specific behavior using a standardized procedure. Behaviors are recorded using frequency, duration, latency (time between the onset of a stimulus and the initiation of the behavior), and time sampling (e.g., 30-minute observation = 120 15-second intervals). This type of observation is more objective than the naturalistic type. For example, you may be asked to observe how often and for how long a student is "on task" (Figure 3).

FIGURE 2: **Sample ABC Chart**

Date	March 10, 2017
Time	11:15 – 11:25 a.m.
How long did behavior last?	30 seconds
What happened prior to the behavior (A)?	Students were assigned independent seat work. The teacher circulated the room to give individual help where needed. The teacher was standing at Tommy's desk.
Specifically describe the behavior (B)	Tommy wads up his worksheet, then tears it up and throws the pieces to the floor.
What was the direct outcome of this behavior (C)?	The other students turn to look at Tommy. The teacher tells Tommy, "Get out another worksheet from my desk and start over." She waits at his desk another 45 seconds.
What happens as a result of these outcomes?	Tommy does not get another worksheet. He sits at his desk looking at the floor.

What does that look like? It means that the student's head and eyes are on the teacher and that the student is participating in teacher-led discussions, has the work area in front of her, follows directions, and is sitting in assigned location. Every 30 minutes, mark whether or not you observe the student "on task." At the end of the observation time, total the number of behaviors and divide them by the total number of intervals to get an overall percentage. Compare this overall percentage to a student who you also observed that does not have a problem behavior of being off task.

FIGURE 3: **Sample Systematic Observation Chart**

Time		Frequency of Target Student Behavior (student who exhibits problem behavior)		Frequency of Control Student Behavior (student who does not exhibit problem behavior)	
0:30		1		1	
1:00		0		1	
1:30		1		1	
2:00		0		1	
		Target Student Totals		**Control Student Totals**	
Category	Total # of Behaviors/ Total # of Intervals	Overall %	Total # of Behaviors/ Total # of Intervals	Overall %	
On Task	2/4	50%	4/4	100%	

This type of data is used to communicate a student's present levels of performance at the beginning of the IEP process as well as a way to monitor a student's progress toward meeting a particular IEP goal. For students who may have goals that are more behavioral in nature, this type of observation is key to showing growth and improvement.

Be an Active Participant

Even if you have some questions or concerns about participating in the IEP process, it's important that you come to the table with an acceptance and willingness to actively participate. Part of this willingness includes keeping an open mind when it comes to trying new approaches. Remember that one of the reasons this student has an IEP is because the traditional general education classroom experience is not working; a new, different approach on the part of the student's stakeholders is precisely what is needed.

Active participation also means asking for additional assistance when you need it. You do not have all of the answers about how best to meet the needs of your students on IEPs, so raise your hand and ask for help. We'll talk more about how to collaborate with other professionals in "Embrace Teamwork" (p. 31). For now, your acceptance and willingness to participate is a must.

The scope of your role in the IEP process is both deep and wide. On the surface there are some technical responsibilities that are required (e.g., anecdotal records, understanding of disability); however, the depth of your role includes your attitudes and beliefs about working with students with disabilities and your willingness to be that all important active participant. It is more than checking a box; it's about changing a life.

2. Tackle All the Necessary Homework for the IEP Meeting

Successful teachers are proactive in their responsibilities of working with students with IEPs. Whether this is your first IEP meeting or part of your annual ritual of IEP reviews, the preparation is the same. It's important not to wait for someone else's direction at this point. Although you might expect a special education teacher will take the lead in soliciting paperwork from you, this might not always be the case. Take an active stance. Be prepared to be prepared.

A vital part of being an active and willing participant in the IEP process is familiarizing yourself with and completing the necessary paperwork and preparation that goes along with this process. Successful teachers know how to describe students' performance, review prior IEP goals, and review their own curriculum, all through the lens of truly understanding the disability category of the IEP.

Take Extra Measures to Describe a Student's Performance Accurately

Each and every time an IEP is developed or reviewed, teachers must provide an account of the student's present levels of performance. In other words, where does he stand right now in their academic career? Complete and up-to-date information on the student's current performance is critical. It is expected that you will report out on all academic areas (i.e., reading, math, writing) of current performance as well as any areas of behavior or cognitive processing that you are responsible for monitoring (e.g., attention, problem solving, communication, social, interpersonal, self-direction). Based on current assessment data, you will be asked to provide statements of current performance in these areas.

One of the teachers I worked with at the middle school level translated performance data into appropriate statements. For example, based on that year's reading fluency testing, she was able to craft an appropriate summary statement about this child's present level of academic performance. One of this student's IEP goals included increasing her oral reading fluency from 12 words correct per minute (WCPM) to at least 80 WCPM by the end of her 1st grade year. After a year of fluency building, the current level of performance of 70 WCPM was reported as "Jessica has increased her oral reading fluency on average of two words per minute. She is reading just below the 75th percentile for grade 1 and struggles with multisyllabic words." This statement combines Jessica's strengths, needs, grade level, and assessment summary.

For each area, develop an appropriate performance statement. As I mentor teachers in this skill, I notice that many statements are vague and not connected to assessment data. For example, the following statements of current performance are at best inappropriate and at worst ineffective:

- Justin is reading below grade level.
- Matthew does not interact appropriately with his peers.
- Mary's handwriting is illegible.

In order to make valid instructional decisions on behalf of students, the summary statements must be specific about the students' strengths, needs, grade level, and based on current assessment data. These statements are the foundation on which new IEP goals are developed. Inappropriate summary statements translate into inappropriate IEP goals.

Review Any Prior IEP Goals

When the baton has been passed to you to care for a child with an IEP, prior goals come with it. Most likely you may have taken either one stand-alone course in IEP planning or those skills were embedded in a course on special education during your teacher preparation. That may not be enough to help you discern whether or not the IEP goals you are now reviewing are appropriate. Because you will be involved in developing new IEP goals for your students, it is imperative that you learn how to evaluate current goals, revise, and create new ones.

Evaluate the prior IEP goals according to the following criteria:

- Are they **individualized**? In other words, are they developed based on the individual student's learning needs based on the assessment data presented in their current levels of performance?

- Are they **aligned** to content standards? The expectation is that students with IEPs will have access to the general curriculum. What that means is that their goals will be developed with the content standards in mind. There should be standards language included in each IEP goal.
- Are they **measurable**? Within each IEP goal there should be an outlined way to measure a student's progress. Does the goal explicitly state how progress toward that goal will be measured?
- Do they include **evidence-based practices** as instructional strategies? A relevant instructional strategy should be mentioned as part of the IEP goal.

An appropriate IEP goal that includes all of these criteria might look like this:

> Given 4th grade level informational texts, Jane will use the PALS strategy to explain their understanding of the texts at least 85 percent of the time by May 30, 2017 as measured by a teacher created comprehension measure.

An IEP goal spans the entire academic year. Short-term objectives for each IEP goal are often then developed to provide measurable benchmarks for the student.

Review Your Curriculum

Part of the preparation of a successful teacher to work with students with IEPs is to take an inventory of their curriculum to ensure that they have in place materials and instructional strategies that are evidence-based. One of the expectations outlined in both IDEIA and the Elementary and Secondary Education Act (ESEA) is that teachers choose and use curricula and instructional practices based on "scientifically-based research" whenever possible. The expectation is clear; however, the practice is questionable. Not all teachers take the time and effort to identify and select curricula and instructional strategies that are evidence-based. In order to work successfully with students with IEPs, meeting this expectation is crucial.

One 4th grade teacher I worked with, Theresa, struggled to prepare for this aspect of the IEP meeting. She was asked to bring a list of curricula and practices that matched the goals of her students with IEPs. At the meeting parents are encouraged to question whether there is evidence that supports the academic, social, or behavioral practices either being proposed or currently used with students. Theresa had inherited this child's IEP that noted activities and assessments, not evidence-based curricula or instructional strategies. She realized she couldn't follow suit; she needed to provide the research-based interventions and appropriate measures in order to meet the goals on this IEP.

Once you've taken an inventory of your curriculum and instructional strategies, you may discover that you need to select additional or different evidence-based practices. The following resources offer information on evidence-based practices:

- What Works Clearinghouse: http://ies.ed.gov/ncee/wwc/
- Promising Practices Network: www.promisingpractices.net
- Center for Evidence-Based Practices: www.evidencebasedpractices.org
- Center for Parent Information and Resources: www.parentcenterhub.org/?s=evidence+based+practices
- The IRIS Center: http://iris.peabody.vanderbilt.edu/ebp_summaries

Prepare for the IEP meeting by aligning your curriculum and instructional strategies to the outlined IEP goals. Show that what you are teaching and how you are teaching supports the needs of the child with the IEP.

Understand the Disability Category

An IEP operates as an instructional tool in the way that it outlines the services provided to the student. The present levels of performance, the IEP goals and short-term objectives, and evidence-based curricula and instructional strategies recommended are all determined and ultimately tied to the disability definition for which the student has been categorized. As a teacher who will work directly to support one or more students with IEPs in your classroom, it's important that you understand the disability categories represented. For example, if you knew that many students with a specific learning disability struggle with written language problems and struggle to develop their fluency (Learning Disabilities

Association of America, n.d.), then it would be appropriate to select curricula and instructional strategies that focus on writing fluency. In addition, you would ensure that if the data reveals that this student indeed struggles with written language, appropriate written language IEP goals were developed.

If, on the other hand, you are not well-versed about the different disability categories represented by the students with IEPs in your classroom, you may make instructional decisions based on faulty information. You will not then be able to enable the student to make progress during the academic year. At the end of the year during the next IEP annual review, you will realize that few, if any, of the student's IEP goals were met. This misalignment impedes progress.

If you realize that you do not understand the disability categories represented in your class, there are several ways to change that.

- **Consult with the special education teacher.** Most likely the special education teacher holds more responsibility for implementing the students' IEPs (Bateman & Bateman, 2006) at your school. As such, she has valuable knowledge and insights into each disability category and recommendations for what works with particular types of students.

- **Confer with current and past teachers.** Teachers who have previously worked with your students have a great deal of insight into the child's disability category and what worked as well as what didn't. Tap into that rich source of information for your own benefit and that of your students. When I taught 6th grade science, I had a child on the autism spectrum in my classroom. I had never before worked with a child on the spectrum, and there was little to no information in her file to help me unlock her challenges. Although a highly gifted learner, the student had both emotional outbursts and frequent off-task behavior when asked to work cooperatively or individually. She was new to the school, and none of her teachers had a history with her. I conferred with both the special education teacher and her 5th grade teachers to discover the nuances of how to work with her successfully. I had to learn how to structure the learning environment with more gentle transitions and provide more one-on-one support even though it wasn't outlined on her IEP. Even as an educator there are times we need to admit we don't know everything, raise our hand with a question, and get help from the experts.

- **Research the disability categories.** No one expects teachers to know everything about every disability category. Even special educators have to review the definitions, characteristics, and educational needs of the categories represented on their caseloads. Successful teachers build a professional library, both on the shelf and online. Sources of this type of information include the following:
    - Federal and state disability definitions: www.idea .ed.gov

- Council for Exceptional Children: www.cec.sped.org
- Disability specific organizations (e.g., www.council-for-learning-disabilities.org)
- A list of recommended books about special education: www.ldonline.org/profbooks/c658

3. Gain a Solid Understanding of What *Modification* and *Accommodation* Mean for an IEP

The underlying principle of an IEP is individualization. Each should be developed and deployed taking into consideration a child's unique needs, strengths, behaviors, and skills. Successful teachers differentiate planning, instruction, and assessment in response to an IEP using a variety of tools (e.g., accommodations, modifications). The next piece of the puzzle is to understand the role that functional academics (e.g., has good work habits, attends to assigned tasks) play in differentiation and meeting the goals on an IEP. Finally, successful teachers know how well students are performing on their IEP goals as far as their class is concerned. Each piece to this puzzle may be unique, but they fit together perfectly.

Define Modification and Accommodation

There are several places on the IEP that require teachers to identify and select how they will work differently with a student so that he may access the general curriculum successfully. For example, under a section titled "Supplementary Aids and Services/Program Modifications/Accommodations" you would outline whether and to what extent aids, services, and other supports are needed to help a student with a disability be educated alongside their nondisabled peers to the maximum extent possible. The difference between modifications and accommodations is often misunderstood. They are not one in the same, nor are the terms interchangeable.

Modifications are needed for students for whom circumstances or conditions severely limit their learning through traditional means. They require specialized instruction that is presented at their cognitive level. What this means is that they may be in 7th grade but they are working at a 3rd grade level. The instructional materials and strategies should be modified to fit their cognitive level. The following areas may need modification:

- **Presentation of subject matter.** The curriculum already chosen for your classroom may need to be modified. You will have to select a curriculum that is specialized for the type of disability and written at a lower level of understanding.
- **Materials and equipment.** Use of assistive technology may be a necessary way to modify either texts or other

learning materials. Use of apps or tablets that provide simplified content in vocabulary, concepts, and principles is effective. The use of a Picture Exchange Communication System (PECS) to simplify demands of both expressive and receptive language of students with struggles in this area is another common modification. Some examples of assistive technology in the classroom include talking calculators, electronic worksheets, word prediction software, text-to-voice devices and software, free-form databases, digital pens, speech recognition technology, and audiobooks.

- **Grading.** A modification of grading generally means to change the weights of assessments. It could also mean to give more formative assessments in lieu of one final summative assessment.

- **Assignments.** Even if assignments are centered on grade-level topics and expectations, you can modify them by lowering the reading level, adapting any worksheets by adding more visual representations, and simplifying vocabulary.

- **Testing adaptations.** Testing modifications may include reducing the reading level of the test or providing an alternative form of the test that simplifies instructions and items. This is appropriate for teacher-made tests.

Accommodations are more appropriate for students who have a recognized disability but are served in the general education or inclusive classroom setting. Accommodations are provided to students with IEPs or those on 504 Plans to remove any barriers to the general curriculum. Accommodations are more common than modifications. The following areas may need accommodations:

- **Pacing.** How often and how long a particular activity requires is pacing. You may extend or adjust the timing, give breaks, or vary the type of activity.
- **Physical environment.** Rearranging the room, minimizing distractions, and providing a support person in the classroom are all examples of this type of accommodation.
- **Presentation of subject matter.** IDEIA recommends Universal Design for Learning (UDL) as a way to provide access to the general education curriculum for students with disabilities. In order to remove barriers to learning, you can vary how the materials used are presented along with your instructional strategies to take advantage of multiple pathways of learning (e.g., visual, auditory, tactile).
- **Materials and equipment.** You may have to find ways to make the content more accessible by providing alternatives like recording texts, note-taking assistance, large print materials, digital alternatives, special equipment for communication, or the use of a computer, tablet, or smartphone for expression of learning.

- **Grading.** Provide multiple means of expression for assessments and give credit for projects and active participation.
- **Assignments.** Accommodations for assignments includes providing smaller, step-by-step instructions, providing oral versus written instructions, adjusting the length or changing the format of the assignment, and even avoiding penalizing for spelling errors on every assignment if that is not the focus of the assignment.
- **Reinforcement and follow through.** Students with IEPs may struggle with organizational skills and other executive functioning skills (e.g., working memory, planning and prioritizing, task initiation, and organization). Accommodate these needs by using positive reinforcement, checking frequently for understanding, requesting parent reinforcement, and conferring with students on a daily or weekly basis.
- **Testing adaptations.** You may also provide additional testing adaptations in your day-to-day working. For example, you could read the test to the student, shorten the length of the test, change the test's format, permit oral answers, permit open book testing, or even allow the student to take the test in an isolated or different location.

Review Any Previously Recommended Accommodations or Modifications

If the student already has an IEP, most likely there are previously noted accommodations or modifications. It's important to review these to ensure that they were appropriate and effective. Successful teachers review prior recommended accommodations before determining their own.

When using an IEP template or an online IEP generator such as IEP Direct, pull-down menus are provided to help teachers select accommodations or modifications. It's important to determine whether the prior accommodations based on learning difficulties are outlined in the present levels of performance statement and whether these accommodations need to be changed.

Determine the Student's Strengths, Weaknesses, Behaviors, and Social Skills

Based on your interaction with the student with an IEP, you are in a position to be able to report on that student's strengths, weaknesses, behaviors, and social skills in your classroom. These descriptors will be included in the child's IEP and become part of adequate planning for annual goals. Whether you teach at the elementary or secondary level, whether you teach a content area or a special, you have data to support the child's state of each of these descriptors.

Strengths and weaknesses are normally reported based on data you've collected throughout the school year on a child's performance. A combination of assessment and anecdotal data helps to paint the portrait of this student. All teachers who work with the student will provide their own insights to the profile of the learner. Students may exhibit different strengths, weaknesses, behaviors, and social skills in different learning environments. That, in and of itself, is important to know when planning goals, curricula, and interventions for students.

Successful teachers predetermine how and to what extent they collect data on a student's performance in anticipation of providing a balanced profile to the IEP team. Consider how a 9th grade social studies teacher, Joann, keeps track of one of her students who had an IEP with reading comprehension and writing goals (Figure 4). Joann first identifies learning targets and how those targets are measured, then notes what the student understands and does well and where he continues to struggle. Common errors, confusions, and even need for greater challenge are observations to capture.

This is one example of how to monitor a student's strengths, weaknesses, behaviors, and social skills. How you monitor these issues is not as important as ensuring that you do. Find a way that works for your teaching style and schedule.

Inventory Functional Academic Skills

Students need functional academic skills for academic success. How often these behaviors occur is important for teachers to know as they begin to plan for meeting IEP goals. For example, use of time, following teacher directions, and attending to tasks are academic skills. Once you take an

FIGURE 4: **Sample Learning Targets**

What is the learning target?	Josh will provide an accurate summary of how key events develop over the course of a text.
Describe student progress toward the learning target.	Josh has increased his ability to accurately summarize from 55 percent correct key events to 70 percent correct key events over six weeks.
List what the student understands or does well (strengths).	Josh is able to identify main chapter events consistently.
List what the student still struggles with or needs greater challenge (struggles).	Josh still has difficulty identifying sub events (details) to create an accurate summary. Common errors include not able to finish assignment in provided time.
What assessment data was used to determine progress?	Chapter outlining assessment = 70 percent correct key events.
What is the next instructional decision?	Change instructional strategy to focus on identifying sub events (details).

inventory of functional academic skills, you can use that data to help you develop both IEP goals and instructional or behavior strategies.

There are a variety of inventories available to guide your inquiry. The skills listed typically fall into the following categories:

- **Time management:** Works within time limits or deadlines, uses free time wisely, or does homework
- **Task management:** Works independently, checks work before handing it in, or completes tasks or activities
- **Listening/following directions:** Listens carefully to teacher instructions, raises hand before speaking, or follows classroom or school rules
- **Quality work:** Makes necessary corrections on assignments without frustration, comes prepared, or performs to ability in reading
- **Effective communication:** Participates in class discussion, asks for help when needed, or performs to ability in written language
- **Social-emotional:** Feels comfortable about being in school, maintains eye contact when speaking or being spoken to, or gets attention in appropriate ways

Based on these kinds of functional academic skills, you can then summarize the student's strengths, weaknesses, and what you believe the student needs in order to be successful.

Know How Students Are Performing on Goals Relevant to Your Class

At this point you've taken the time to familiarize yourself with what it truly means to accommodate your materials, curricula, and instruction to the needs of your students on IEPs. You understand what academic skills they need in order to be successful in your class. You have contributed to the design of their IEP goals and know what their present levels of performance include. Going forward it will be crucial to know unequivocally how well they are performing toward the goals set forth in your class. Do you have a plan to monitor their progress?

How well students are progressing in your class flows naturally from the goals developed from the IEP. You've already indicated how that goal will be measured, so the key is to use frequent and brief measures on a regular basis to see how they are doing. The idea is to assess what you are teaching, not teaching to a test. Using curriculum-based measures (CBMs) is a research-based approach to monitoring student progress toward their IEP goals and to see how they are doing in your classroom. Using CBMs helps you to evaluate the success of the instruction the child is receiving, provides results in scores that are easy to understand and communicate, and is time efficient. Take a look at the following IEP goals and their companion measures of progress:

- Measurable IEP annual goal: Given a 2nd grade reading passage, Jess will read 150 wpm with 95 percent accuracy over five consecutive sessions.
  - How progress will be measured: Jess will read orally for one minute per week. The teacher will observe and document the number of words and errors.

- Measurable IEP annual goal: Given 7th grade real world mathematical problems involving the four operations with rational numbers, Kevin will use the Paraphrasing Strategy to solve word problems with 95 percent accuracy over six consecutive sessions.
  - How progress will be measured: Kevin will apply the Paraphrasing Strategy to four grade level word problems each week. The teacher will observe and document the number of correct answers and errors.

How you can successfully measure student progress toward their IEP goals will be more thoroughly addressed in "Stay on Top of Student Progress" (p. 42).

4. Embrace Teamwork

Successful teachers know that working with and on behalf of students with IEPs is a collaborative process, not a solo performance. We are a crucial member of the orchestra and as such need to know both how to play our parts well and how our part plays into the whole of the concerto. This section offers ways in which teachers can learn their parts and be open to collaboration on behalf of the children in their care to include co-teaching, working with case managers, and even seeking teaching demonstrations.

Successful collaboration for the sake of students, especially for those who struggle, depends on a variety of factors. Willingness to collaborate is the foundational factor. Successful teachers reject the lone ranger approach to teaching and instead embrace teamwork. Both special education and general education teachers bring something of value to the table. General education teachers may not be familiar with specialized instruction used in special education or how to match practice with a child's skill level especially if they are far below grade level. Special education teachers may not be as familiar with the various learning activities or projects often used to demonstrate learning on grade level. Both know techniques to deal with disciplinary problems or motivation challenges. Finding common ground is an integral part of collaboration, but capitalizing on each other's strengths is just as necessary.

Work with Case Manager to Implement IEP

Special education teachers at your school carry a caseload. That means they are responsible and accountable for the progress of a group of students with IEPs in your school or grade level. At the elementary level they may operate as a consultant to a teacher who monitors the progress of a student who has been completely mainstreamed, provide intensive intervention to those at the highest risk of failing, or maintain a resource classroom or self-contained special education classroom for those with more needs. At the secondary level they may also act as a consultant teacher, act as a co-teacher, or teach a special education section of an academic area. Both levels of special education teachers are intimately connected to students' IEPs and the management of their learning. As such they are the best people to consult as you attempt to implement a student's IEP.

Making decisions about the instruction for and implementation of a child's IEP should and can be done together. The *Five Step Process* (Minnesota Department of Children, Families, and Learning, Division of Special Education, 2002) outlines an effective strategy for doing so:

1. Review the standard, performance task, IEP goal, and curricular demands. General education and special education teachers communicate about the goal and standard students will be working toward.

2. Discuss the learning needs of the student and the availability of resources. Teachers take the time to talk about the student's specific needs and concerns relevant to the classroom placement or setting. Discuss accommodations or modifications.

3. Decide on accommodations for the student and decide who will be responsible for implementing them. Teachers work together to find creative ways to allow the student to more fully participate in the instruction and access the general curriculum.

4. Monitor, adjust, and provide formative feedback. Teachers work together to determine who will be responsible for monitoring the effectiveness of the accommodation(s) implemented.

5. Evaluate students using established criteria.
Teachers work together to identify learning targets and discuss in what ways students will be evaluated in relation to those targets.

Ask for Demonstrations of the Accommodations

Once you have collaborated with the special education teacher about appropriate accommodations for a particular student with an IEP, you may discover that implementing what's on paper isn't as easy as it seems. Intellectually you may understand what it means to level the social studies texts to the child's reading level, but what does that really look like in practice? Successful teachers ask for demonstrations of different accommodations from those already proficient in the practice. When you take the time to observe how something is done well, you are more apt to embrace and repeat it for your own professional practice. Seek advice and demonstrations from the experts in the field. Keep in mind that the students themselves are experts on what accommodations work for them and how they can be implemented.

Here are some tips for learning how to incorporate needed accommodations:

- **Take the lead in your own learning.** If you notice an accommodation on a child's IEP that you are not familiar with, seek out help. Don't wait for another professional to walk you through it; take responsibility for your own learning. Check with previous teachers, a special education teacher, or even students about how to implement an accommodation.

- **Be a focused observer.** Whether you learn how to implement an accommodation during a training workshop or at the hands of another teacher, focus on how well the accommodation will work in your particular classroom with your particular classroom dynamics. Ask reflective questions about the implementation that show your awareness of the needs of your students.
- **Be an active participant.** While observing how to implement an accommodation, work with the one modeling to apply the practice immediately. Don't remain passive as a learner; be active.

If you discover a dearth of available demonstrators for accommodations in your school or district, be on the hunt for resources outside of your immediate area. There are demonstrations of accommodations online that combine the "show" with the "tell." Successful teachers do not allow the lack of support or resources to define their effectiveness. They are persistent hunters and gatherers in search of what works.

Be Open to Co-Development of IEP Goals

In order to create a climate that is conducive to supporting the success of all students, become an integral part of the ongoing communication needed to co-develop students' IEP goals. Because there are more and more students being educated in an inclusive classroom setting, all teachers need to be aware of the goals and objectives on IEPs. When you have a hand in developing these IEP goals, you can help determine what a student can reasonably be expected to do during the 12-month period of the IEP. Whether you hold all or part of the instructional responsibility to ensure that students with IEPs access the curriculum, start with the end in mind (IEP goals) before beginning to plan instruction.

Consider these practices when working to co-develop IEP goals with a special education teacher:

- **Bring your knowledge of how the student with an IEP performs in your context.** Before you can effectively develop an IEP goal you will need to know and provide information about your context and how well the student is working within that context. Consider how the student interacts with her peers, responds to the pace of the class, responds to the dynamics of the class, and responds to other students in the class. This will be helpful to the special education teacher as you both work to come up with appropriate IEP goals.

- **Ensure that IEP goals are aligned to standards.** In most cases the general education teacher is the subject matter expert in this partnership. Because the IEP is the driving force in a student's education, it is important that any IEP goals that are academically focused are aligned to whatever standards the school or district uses. This ensures that they will be relevant to the general education teacher and classroom and that grade level progress will be monitored appropriately.

- **Brainstorm ways to meet IEP goals prior to final development.** This is where the tactical and the strategic meet. The goals are the long-term strategic thinking, but the ways in which you will help students meet those goals is tactical. Together with the special education teacher, talk about different instructional strategies and curricula choices that offer students with IEPs specific and individual ways to meet their goals. This upfront work will better position both teachers and students in this endeavor.

- **Center your conversations on instruction and student learning.** It is tempting to find reasons to complain about having to differentiate your instruction for the sake of a diverse learner because it will create more work for you as a teacher. However, this type of conversation is not effectual or transformational for yourself as a teacher or the students in your care. When you meet with other professionals about the needs of a student with an IEP, focus your thoughts and words on the following: the child's strengths, needs, progress, and areas of concern. This will keep you in problem-solving mode and not problem-making mode.

- **Maintain a familiarity with each student's goals.** In order to provide students with ample opportunities to work on their IEP goals and ensure that your instructional supports are provided consistently, it's important to become very familiar with students' goals and outline opportunities to address them. Sometimes opportunities occur naturally during ongoing instruction, while at other times you need to be intentional and embed specific supports or instructional strategies. Plan carefully with the special education teacher to ensure that students' needs are met.

John, a 6th grade student, is struggling with reading comprehension. His teacher keeps track of what, when, where, and how his IEP goal will be implemented in the following way:

- **IEP Goal.** John will increase comprehension of a variety of printed material to 90 percent accuracy as measured by DIBELS ORF Retell by May 30.
- **Objective 1.** Locate information and clarify meaning by skimming, scanning, reading carefully, and using other reading strategies.
- **Objective 2.** Use word attack strategies to locate specific words, phrases, and word patterns and recognize sight words when returning to familiar text.
- **Goal Implementation in the Following Classes**
    - ☑ ELA (Language Arts)
    - ☑ Math
    - ☑ Science
    - ☑ Social Studies

Jessica, a 9th grade student, has difficulty in written expression. Her teacher keeps track of what, when, where, and how her IEP goal will be implemented in the following way:

- **IEP Goal.** Jessica will increase writing skills to grade level in the areas of sentence fluency and conventions as measured by an analysis of writing samples by May 30.
- **Objective 1.** Write clear, focused main ideas and supporting details
- **Objective 2.** Write a multi-paragraph passage to develop a topic using details, examples, and illustrations.
- Goal Implementation in the Following Classes
  - ☑ English (Language Arts)
  - ☐ Algebra
  - ☑ Science
  - ☑ Social Studies

Try Co-Teaching

Whether you find yourself in an integrated co-teaching classroom, or you simply need more training in how to select and implement instructional strategies and routines that are evidence-based in order to meet students' IEP goals, making the choice to co-teach will support you and your students. Working alongside a special educator complements your content knowledge with the specialized instruction required by an IEP. If, for example, the IEP dictates that multisensory instruction is expected to meet a reading fluency goal, do you know how to plan for an execute the multisensory approach to reading? We often ignore those skills at which we are not proficient; however, ignoring a needed instructional strategy or approach does nothing to improve your confidence or a student's competence.

Students with IEPs belong to both general educators and special educators, so both must be informed about the requirements of the IEP for each student in their care. Together you can work toward meeting those goals and ensure adequate progress toward them during the school year (Bauer & Kroeger, 2004). If this type of collaboration is not required in your school, that doesn't mean it can't be voluntary. As you consider co-teaching, keep the following models in mind along with the strengths and weaknesses of each.

- **Station teaching.** Both the special educator and the general educator teach through learning centers. Although each teacher is responsible for delivering part of the lesson, it requires extensive planning in advance.
- **Parallel teaching.** After dividing the class in two, the special educator and the general educator deliver the same lesson to their groups at the same time. Although this is an efficient approach and allows each teacher to use strategies tailored for each group, it may be noisy and create labeled groups (e.g., slow or advanced).
- **Alternative teaching.** One teacher, either the general educator or the special educator, teaches using whole-class instruction while the other teaches using small-group instruction. Although this approach allows for re-teaching of specific skills in the smaller

group, it should not last for the entire class time. Negative labeling can occur if the same students are pulled regularly.

- **Team teaching.** Both the general educator and the special educator deliver instruction at the same time and naturally shift roles between leading whole class, observing instruction, and checking for student understanding. Although both teachers play an active role and are viewed as equally in charge, this requires the most planning and communication, as well as being comfortable with each other and each of your styles.

- **One teach, one assist.** Most often this is where the general educator delivers instruction while the special educator circulates through the class providing assistance to students when needed. Although this approach offers individual students "just in time" support, special educators are often viewed as non-teachers by the students and sometimes by the general education teacher, and their instructional strategies and knowledge of disabilities and how to meet IEP goals are underused by their co-teachers.

Your school may dictate which co-teaching model to employ, however, you are encouraged to use what is in the best interest of the students in your class. You don't have to choose one model over another; you can use different models for different purposes throughout the day. Learn from one another how best to meet the needs of students on IEPs. Here are some suggested resources:

- Accommodations Finder: www.interventioncentral .org/teacher-resources/learning-disability-accommodations-finder
- Working Together: Science Teachers and Students with Disabilities: www.washington.edu/doit/videos/ index.php?vid=34

5. Stay on Top of Student Progress

Successful teachers do not wait for the results of a district or statewide assessment; they use a variety of measures to both check frequently and formatively for student understanding and progress toward meeting any IEP goals that are a part of their class. This section describes how to use IEP goals in instructional planning, how to create appropriate benchmarks, and ways to probe for progress. As often as progress should be communicated, successful teachers create student profiles to share with all stakeholders including parents.

Use IEP Goals During Instructional Planning

One of the questions I always ask teachers in trainings is "How do you use IEP goals to plan your instruction?" Often the answers range from "Am I supposed to?" to "I don't."

This is problematic because in inclusive settings the general education teacher holds the primary instructional responsibility for the students with disabilities in their classrooms. Successful teachers plan instruction with the needs of their students in mind. For students on IEPs, their educational needs are outlined through annual goals and objectives. The following ideas need to be a part of your instructional planning toolbox:

- **Use your content expertise to align goals to standards**. Although special education teachers need to learn how to harness the Common Core or state content area standards in order to develop appropriate IEP goals and be valuable contributors to planning, instruction, and assessment, general educators must ensure that those IEP goals are aligned to standards and therefore relevant to the curriculum they use in their classrooms. For example, if a student needs a goal to improve their writing and they are in an inclusive 5th grade classroom, you can recommend that the IEP writing goal align to standards as "Student will summarize or paraphrase information in notes and finished work, and provide a list of sources for a research project by May 2017" (based on CCSS.ELA-LITERACY.W5.8).
- **Plan instruction with Universal Design for Learning (UDL) in mind.** Although general educators are prepared in the Common Core or state content area standards, they may not be prepared in differentiating their instruction for diverse learners to provide access

to the general curriculum to students with IEPs. During the pre-planning stage of instruction, consider how you will provide multiple means of representation, engagement, and expression. For students with IEPs, especially those with significant disabilities, assistive technology is a primary way to provide the student with multiple means of engaging with the content and demonstrating their understanding of that content. Include the use of assistive technology in your lesson planning. For more information and examples of how to plan instruction with UDL in mind, access the UDL modules for elementary, secondary, and adapted curriculum at the MAST website at http://mast.ecu.edu/picker.php.

- **Design individual accommodations within lesson plans.** Once you have aligned the standards to the goals and determined how to apply UDL to your instructional planning, you will be able to include specific accommodations for each student with an IEP in your lesson plans. For some this task may seem overwhelming at first. The following tips will make this accessible for both you and your students:
  - Review the students' IEPs to ensure that the expected lesson modifications or accommodations listed are appropriate for your content area.
  - Create an individual custom accommodations checklist for each student with an IEP in your class (Gould & Vaughn, 2000).

- Include students' strengths and interests in lesson changes to create more accessible and engaging lessons.
- Provide additional practice opportunities for students within lessons.
- Scaffold the instruction by breaking the lesson into smaller pieces of information.
- Include modeling of skills to students as often as possible.

For more specific accommodations, see the "Accommodations Checklist" on the ASCD website: www.ascd.org/ASCD/pdf/books/caruana2017.pdf.

Include Evaluation Methods in Lesson Plans

Based on the evaluation information provided in the IEP, successful teachers determine ways in which they will evaluate student progress and include those ways in the lesson plan. Consider evaluating progress in a variety of ways beyond a traditional paper/pencil test. Check for understanding by asking questions, monitoring student work, facilitating discussions, and assessing student products according to the benchmarks that you've previously determined (Gould & Vaughn, 2000).

If, for example, a goal for a student in your 10th grade English class states "Given a topic, the student will compose a five-paragraph essay in which each will include a topic sentence, at least three supporting details, and logical sequence by May 2017," divide the condition into six benchmarks (one for each grading period of the year) with increasing difficulty in order to meet the goal by year's end. Then evaluate the students' progress toward the goal by monitoring their progress during each lesson or unit. You can devise a curriculum-based measure (CBM) to assess student progress toward their goal. In this way you include an appropriate method of evaluation for a student with an IEP in your lesson plans.

Reflect on Your Teaching Effectiveness

It's crucial to determine whether or not all of your effort on behalf of a student with an IEP has been effective or not. Frequent reflection on its effectiveness can help you make course corrections when necessary. After collecting and graphing your students' data, you will be able to see how close to their goals they are progressing. Successful teachers monitor student progress frequently. If the IEP states that each goal is assessed every week, then you will monitor a student's progress every week. As often as you assess, remember that you are not only assessing the student's progress but also your own. Determining how you will reflect on your teaching effectiveness before you even start will make that process an integral part of your teaching. Consider noting the following information each time you assess a student's progress:

- **Learning target.** Identify the specific learning objectives and learning targets measured by the assessment (probe) you chose for analysis.

- **Student progress.** Create a graphic (table or chart) or narrative that summarizes student learning for your students.
- **Consider what students understand and do well, and where they continue to struggle.** Identify common errors, confusions, or need for greater challenge.
- **Patterns of learning.** Analyze student work to identify the patterns of learning relative to the essential skill or strategy being taught.
- **Next steps.** Ask yourself how you will adjust your teaching based on the student's progress so far.

When you analyze student learning, you are also analyzing your teaching effectiveness. It's always better to ask yourself what kind of impact you are having on student learning before someone else does.

Create Student Profiles to Share

Because your work with students on IEPs is a collaborative effort, you will need to find ways to share students' progress with all the stakeholders. For example, you will report student progress to the IEP team in a formal manner. You will also need to share student progress or lack thereof with other teachers and parents. Each of these reports may require a different format, but they all include similar elements. Creating a student profile for each of your students may seem like a daunting task, but it is well worth the effort in the end. At the end of each school year you can create a profile that can be shared with the next year's teachers. It can also be used as evidence of your impact on student learning.

The elements included in a student profile may include, but are not limited to, the following:

- Student name
- Grade and teacher
- Dates of interventions
- Baseline data
- Learning targets and IEP goals
- Assessment used
- Instructional strategy used
- Graph of progress
- Statement of progress
- Strengths, interests, and concerns
- Recommendations

This type of profile can be captured in one to two pages at most. It is a profile and not a report. The recommendations you include at the end should be applied to the next teacher. You can and should use what you gained from your reflection on teaching effectiveness to determine next steps for the student you are profiling.

When you take the data you've collected (the what) and interpret that data for the student's strengths and struggles (the so what), you can then make instructional decisions and recommendations on behalf of that student (the now what). The exercise changes from a technical one to a transformative one—for both your students and yourself as a teacher.

Conclusion

Although it is difficult to be prepared for every eventuality with such a diverse set of students, successful teachers take the initiative to become better prepared and engage in lifelong learning. The skills needed to effectively implement IEPs are not a secret; they are evidence-based in both the research literature and in practice. As the inclusive classroom becomes the placement of choice for many students with disabilities, the implementation of a student's IEP is no longer the sole responsibility of a special education teacher. Together the general education teacher and the special education teacher work to ensure each student's progress toward meeting their carefully crafted goals.

Although the steps in this process may change over time when the IEP process changes, the foundational skills presented in this book can be adapted to any shift in process. Becoming informed, being willing to participate, knowing the needs of your students, being transparent in your planning and instruction, and being open to collaboration are all characteristics of highly successful and effective teachers. Apply them to the implementation of IEPs and you will make a positive difference for your students.

To give your feedback on this publication and
be entered into a drawing for a free ASCD
Arias e-book, please visit
www.ascd.org/ariasfeedback

ENCORE

IEP SNAPSHOTS

Elementary IEP Snapshot

Basic Information	**Medical Information**
Student:_____	Diagnosis: _____
ID#:_____	Seizures:
DOB:_____	☐ Yes
End of IEP Date:_____	☐ No
Grade:_____	If yes, plan:_____
Eligibility Category:_____	
	Allergies:
Behavior Plan:	☐ Yes
☐ Yes	☐ No
☐ No	If yes: _____
ESL:	
☐ Yes	Medications & Times:
☐ No	_____
	_____

Related Services	Day	Time(s)
SLP	M T W TH F	
PT	M T W TH F	
OT	M T W TH F	
Adaptive PE	M T W TH F	
Guidance	M T W TH F	

Academic Area	IEP Goal
Reading	
Writing	
Math	

Strengths	Struggles

Accommodations/Modifications

Secondary IEP Snapshot

Student Name:_____	Date of Snapshot:_____
DOB:_____	Date of IEP:_____
Disability:_____	Re-Eval Date:_____
Case Manager:_____	Related Services:_____
Planning Period:_____	

Reading Level:	Written Language:	Math Level:

Strengths/Interests:	Needs/Concerns:

Behavioral Issues:	Communication Issues:	Other Issues:

Accommodations/Modifications		
Supplementary Aids/Services/ Supports	**Amount of Time/ Frequency/ Conditions**	**Location**
Use of calculator/ mult. chart	Daily for all math operations on assignments/ tests/quizzes	For all classes
Extended time/ double time	Available to student daily for assignments/ tests/quizzes	For all classes
Test read	When reading level of test is above student level	For all classes in alternative room
Modify assignments and tests	When reading level of tasks is above student level	For all classes
Use of assistive communication device	When needed	For all classes

Additional Information: _____

_____

_____

References

Archer, A. L., & Hughes, C. A. (2011). *Explicit instruction: Effective and efficient teaching.* New York: Guilford Press.

Avramidis, E., Bayliss, P., & Burden, R. (2000). Student teachers' attitudes towards the inclusion of children with special educational needs in the ordinary school. *Teaching and Teacher Education, 16*(3), 277–293.

Bateman, D., & Bateman, C. F. (2006). *A principal's guide to special education* (2nd ed.). Arlington, VA: Council for Exceptional Children.

Bauer, A. M., & Kroeger, S. (2004). *The inclusive classroom: Strategies for effective instruction.* Upper Saddle River, NJ: Pearson Education.

Cassady, J. M. (2011). Teachers' attitudes toward the inclusion of students with autism and emotional behavioral disorder. *Electronic Journal for Inclusive Education, 2*(7), 1–23.

Gould, A., & Vaughn, S. (2000). Planning for the inclusive classroom: Meeting the needs of diverse learners. *Catholic Education: A Journal of Inquiry and Practice, 3*(3), 363–374.

Individuals with Disabilities Improvement Education Act. Pub. L. No. 108–446, Part B (2004).

Learning Disabilities Association of America. (n.d.). *Types of learning disabilities.* Retrieved from https://ldaamerica.org/types-of-learning-disabilities/

McNulty, R. J., & Gloeckler, L. C. (2011). *Fewer, clearer, higher Common Core State Standards: Implications for students receiving special education services.* Rexford, NY: International Center for Leadership in Education. Retrieved from www.leadered.com/pdf/fewer_clearer_higher_ccss_special_education_2014.pdf

Minnesota Department of Children, Families and Learning, Division of Special Education. (2002). *Five Step Process.* St. Paul, MN: Author.

Samuels, C. A. (2013, October 28). Common Core's promise collides with IEP realities. *Education Week.* Retrieved from www.edweek.org/ew/articles/2013/10/30/10cc-iep.h33.html

Related ASCD Resources

At the time of publication, the following ASCD resources were available (ASCD stock numbers appear in parentheses). For up-to-date information about ASCD resources, go to www.ascd.org. You can search the complete archives of *Educational Leadership* at http://www.ascd.org/el.

ASCD EDge®
Exchange ideas and connect with other educators interested in inclusion on the social networking site ASCD EDge at http://ascdedge.ascd.org.

Print Products
Co-Planning for Co-Teaching: Time-Saving Routines That Work in Inclusive Classrooms (ASCD Arias) by Gloria Lodato Wilson (#SF117018)

Educational Leadership: Co-Teaching: Making It Work (December 2015/January 2016) (#116031)

A Teacher's Guide to Special Education by David F. Bateman & Jenifer L. Cline (#116019)

Teaching in Tandem: Effective Co-Teaching in the Inclusive Classroom by Gloria Lodato Wilson and Joan Blednick (#110029)

For more information: send e-mail to member@ascd.org; call 1-800-933-2723 or 703-578-9600, press 2; send a fax to 703-575-5400; or write to Information Services, ASCD, 1703 N. Beauregard St., Alexandria, VA 22311-1714 USA.

About the Author

Dr. Vicki Caruana is a professor of education at Mount Saint Mary College in New York. She prepares teacher candidates in a dual certification in special education for both the elementary and secondary programs. Caruana also provides professional development in the areas of inclusion, evidence-based practices, and IEP implementation. She has taught at the K–12 level in public schools for both students with disabilities and gifted students. She has authored more than 22 books for both teachers and parents, including the best-selling *Apples & Chalkdust: Inspirational Stories and Encouragement for Teachers*. Caruana has two grown sons, one of whom is also a teacher, and lives with her station wagon-crazy husband, Chip, in Newburgh, New York.